THE HOUSE THAT JACK BUILT

PETEPETOWN

EMETEE

GAVIN BISHOP

BEING The ACCOUNT of JACK BULL Esq who SAILED from these SHORES to a LAND FAR AWAY to LIVE there and TRADE with the NATIVES of that said land 12th DAY of SEPTEMBER 1798

HAATEKE

KOOROOROO

SCHOLASTIC
Auckland Sydney New York London
Toronto Mexico City New Delhi Hong Kong

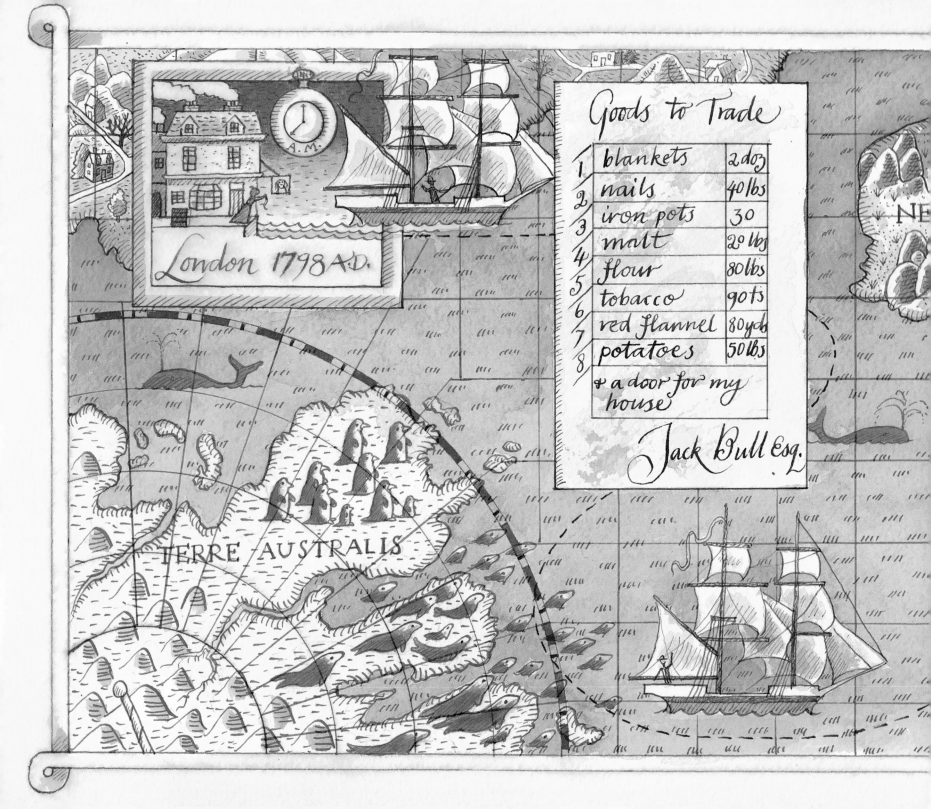

London 1798 A.D.

A.M.

Goods to Trade

1	blankets	2 doz
2	nails	40 lbs
3	iron pots	30
4	malt	20 lbs
5	flour	80 lbs
6	tobacco	9 ots
7	red flannel	80 yds
8	potatoes	50 lbs
	& a door for my house	

Jack Bull Esq.

TERRE AUSTRALIS

NE

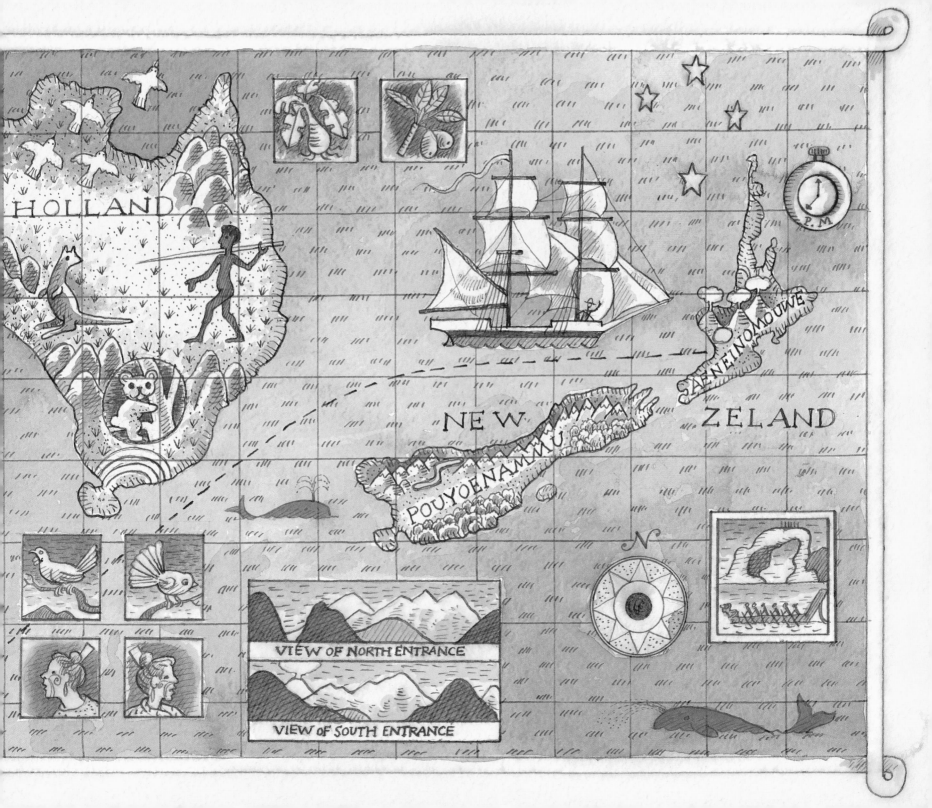

HOLLAND

NEW ZELAND

POUYOENAMMU

AENEINOMOUWE

P.M

N

VIEW OF NORTH ENTRANCE

VIEW OF SOUTH ENTRANCE

6

PAPATUANUKU THE EARTH MOTHER GAVE BIRTH TO ALL LIVING THINGS.

"NO!" SAID TANE MAHUTA, "I WILL SEPARATE THEM." AND HE DID.

This is the **house** that **Jack** built.

ABOUT WHAT TO DO. "KILL THEM!" SAID TUMATAUENGA THE WAR GOD!

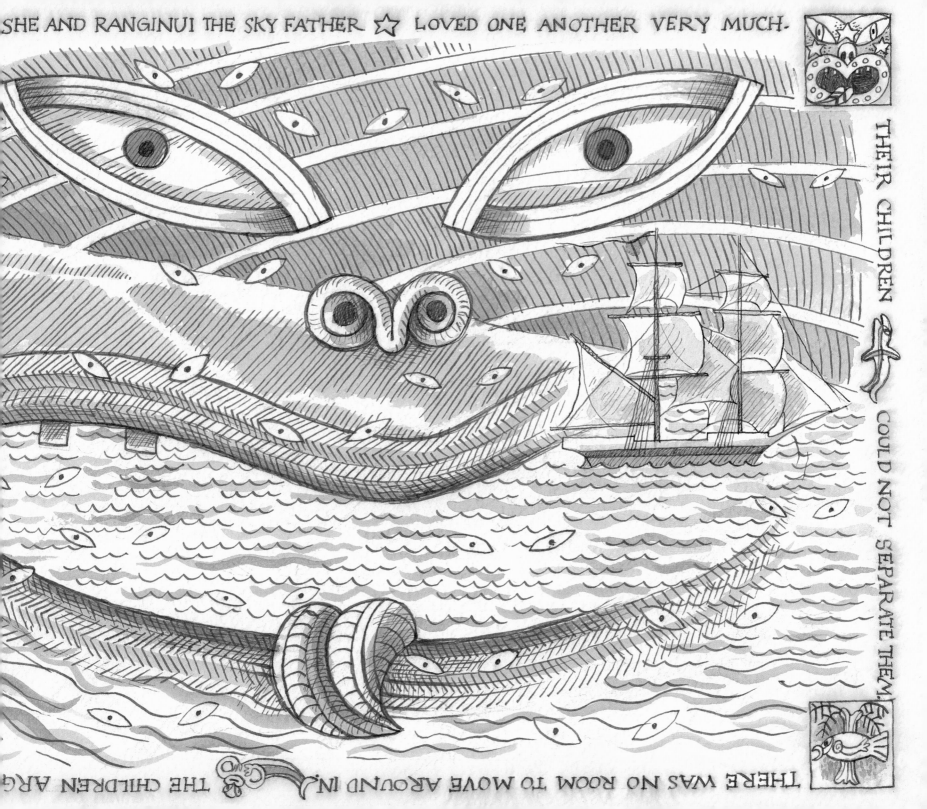

SHE AND RANGINUI THE SKY FATHER ☆ LOVED ONE ANOTHER VERY MUCH.

THEIR CHILDREN COULD NOT SEPARATE THEM.

THERE WAS NO ROOM TO MOVE AROUND IN. THE CHILDREN ARG

Capt Meatrack   2 twists of tobacco   1   6d.
For Am   12 yds rope   1 17   9d.
                           12
Mr W   1 bag malt   15   0
Balance

This is the **malt**,
That **lay** in the house that Jack built.

This is the **rat**,
That **ate** the malt,
That lay in the house that Jack built.

Rev S.   1lb nails   1   0
Stores   1 iron pot   1 12   6
                                               1 13   6

Mrs McKay   1 bag flour   12   6

This is the **cat**,
That **killed** the rat,
That ate the malt,
That lay in the house that Jack built.

This is the **dog**,
That **worried** the cat,
That killed the rat,
That ate the malt,
That lay in the house that Jack built.

Dirty Mey   1 iron whale pot   8 17   9
(to be delivered)   1 harpoon   9 11   5

OR HE COULD LOOK LIKE AN EEL.

This is the **cow** with the **crumpled horn**,
That **tossed** the dog,
That worried the cat,
That killed the rat,
That ate the malt,
That lay in the house that Jack built.

This is the **maiden** all **forlorn**,
That **milked** the cow with the crumpled horn,
That tossed the dog,
That worried the cat,
That killed the rat,
That ate the malt,
That lay in the house that Jack built.

This is the **man** all **tattered** and **torn**,
That **kissed** the maiden all forlorn,
That milked the cow with the crumpled horn,
That tossed the dog,
That worried the cat,
That killed the rat,
That ate the malt,
That lay in the house that Jack built.

This is the **priest** all **shaven** and **shorn**,
That **married** the man all tattered and torn,
That kissed the maiden all forlorn,
That milked the cow with the crumpled horn,
That tossed the dog,
That worried the cat,
That killed the rat,
That ate the malt,
That lay in the house that Jack built.

THERE IS ONLY ONE GOD OUR FATHER IN HEAVEN

Plan of
Jackstown

This is the **cock** that **crowed** in the **morn,**
That **woke** the priest all shaven and shorn,
That married the man all tattered and torn,
That kissed the maiden all forlorn,
That milked the cow with the crumpled horn,
That tossed the dog,
That worried the cat,
That killed the rat,
That ate the malt,
That lay in the house that Jack built.

This is the **farmer** **sowing** his **corn**,

That kept the  that crowed in the morn,

That woke the  all shaven and shorn,

That married the  all tattered and torn, That kissed the  all forlorn,

That milked the  with the crumpled horn, That tossed the

That worried the  That killed the  That ate the

That lay in the  that **Jack** built.

This is the **soldier** all **weary** and **worn,**

AGAIN AND AGAIN TUMATAUENGA, THE WAR GOD

DANCE OF WAR WAS HEARD OVER THE LAND.

And this **was** the house that Jack built.

THE PEOPLE TOOK UP THEIR WEAPONS AND THE TERRIBLE

About This Book

The pictures in this book are a metaphor for what happened when European traders, sealers, whalers and settlers arrived in Aotearoa/New Zealand during the early 19th century.

It is 1798 when Jack Bull Esq. arrives in Aotearoa to find a land strong in spirit and tradition. The Maori, the people of the land, are eager to have his iron pots, nails and blankets to enhance their daily life. But Jack's arrival is followed by more and more people from Europe.

To the Maori, the land is their Earth Mother, Papatuanuku, who gives life to all things. However, the settlers pressure the Maori to give up their land to build farms and towns, and Papatuanuku is divided and sold. Tension over the loss of tribal land, and the failure of the Treaty of Waitangi in 1840 to bind the two peoples together, leads to the Land Wars of the 1860s. Tumatauenga, god of war, calls the Maori people to fight for Papatuanuku. She grows strong once more and her presence fills the page. The remains of the 'house' that Jack built smoulders in the foreground as a symbol of the conflict.

When Jack first builds his house, we see the land, sea and sky dominated by the Earth Mother, Papatuanuku, the Sky Father, Ranginui, and the eyes of their children. They are drawn in a style that reflects traditional Maori art forms.

As the story unfolds and Jack's house continues to grow, the spirit of the Earth Mother weakens and fades. The pictures showing events through the eyes of the Europeans are naturalistic in style, while comments from a Maori perspective run around the borders of the page.

On the last pages the conflict is recorded for future generations on the wall of a meeting house in a folk art style blending traditional Maori and European art forms. Both cultures are now intertwined in the rich history of Aotearoa.

Gavin Bishop
Aotearoa, 1999

"STAND UP! PROTECT THE EARTH MOTHER!

The author gratefully acknowledges the assistance of Creative New Zealand in the publication of this book

First published by Scholastic New Zealand Limited, 1999
Private Bag 94407, Greenmount, Auckland 1730, New Zealand.

Scholastic Australia Pty Limited
PO Box 579, Gosford, NSW 2250, Australia.

Scholastic Inc
555 Broadway, New York, NY 10012-3999, USA.

Scholastic Limited
1-19 New Oxford Street, London, WC1A 1NU, England.

Scholastic Canada Limited
123 Newkirk Road, Richmond Hill, Ontario L4C 3G5, Canada.

Scholastic Mexico
Bretana 99, Col. Zacahuitzco, 03550, Mexico D.F., Mexico.

Scholastic India Pte Limited
29 Udyog Vihar, Phase-1, Gurgaon-122 016, Haryana, India.

Scholastic Hong Kong
Room 601-2, Tung Shung Hing Commercial Centre,
20-22 Granville Road, Kowloon, Hong Kong.

© Gavin Bishop, 1999
ISBN 1-86943-434-X

9 8 7 6 5 4 3 2 1   9 / 9   0 1 2 3 4 / 0

Edited by Frances Chan
Layout by Crispin Schuberth
Typeset in 16/23pt Korinna
Printed in Hong Kong